The Surro Fairy™

Written by
Michelle Minucci

Illustrated by
Winda Lee

Copyright © 2019 by Michelle Minucci
All rights reserved. This book or any portion there of
may not be reproduced or used in any manner whatsoever
without the express written permission of the publisher
except for the use of brief quotations in a book review.

Printed in the United States of America

First Printing, 2019

www.surrofairy.com

For all the magical babies born via surrogacy.

For the mommies and daddies that keep believing.

And, for all the Fairies that help wishes come true.

Far away, in a warm, safe place, there lived a land of Surro Fairies. For as long as any of the fairies could remember, they'd been helping families who wanted a baby to have one.

Mommies and daddies of all kinds would send wishes to the Surro Fairies. Each of the wishes floated in the air until one fairy grabbed them and told the others.

"Look here," said Sarah Surro. "These two daddies would love a little girl."

Chrissie Surro tumbled through the air, excited. "And look, fairies, this mommy and daddy want a little boy! Oh, a boy and a girl. Twins!"

The Surro Fairies giggled and fluttered around their Surro Fairy home. Each of them would be ready to carry a little emby—an embryo—until it grew into a laughing, loveable, and healthy baby.

Maribel Surro took out her tablet and tapped the screen. "Chrissie, take all those messages so I can enter them in the computer. One baby girl, twins—boy and girl, and what else?"

The fairies helped Maribel Surro gather all the wishes from mommies and daddies. Soon, they had a long list of new embies.

And then, far away, in a busy city, there was a mommy-to-be who sat down in a chair. She looked out the window at the tall buildings, trees, and the sun as it began to set.

The last light of day made her think of her own mommy who rocked her to sleep when she was little.

"I just want to be a mommy, too," she said.

"Here," someone said.

Mommy-to-be turned to see her husband, a daddy-to-be. He had his phone out, and an app was open on the screen: "SURRO FAIRY: BABY WISHES FOR ALL TYPES OF MOMMIES AND DADDIES."

Mommy-to-be's name was Vanessa and daddy-to-be was Noah.

Noah said, "We can look on this app for the perfect Surro Fairy. We can find the one that suits us best. Maybe she loves to read and sing, or maybe she's interested in science and sports."

Vanessa gently held Noah's hand and said "Maybe she's looking for the perfect match too."

Noah laughed. "We pick her out here, our Surro Fairy gets the message, and they get the little emby ready to go."

"Little emby?"

"The little *embryo* that grows into a baby."

Vanessa and Noah, along with their friends Hugo and Peter, all wanted to be mommies and daddies. But, each of them couldn't right now: Vanessa's doctor said she needed a Surro Fairy—and so did Hugo and Peter's doctor.

Everyone agreed the Surro Fairies would be the answer.

"So, we pick out our little baby here, and the Surro Fairies deliver her?" asked Hugo.

"That's right," said Noah. "Well, sort of. We pick out a fairy first."

Together, the families-to-be picked out their babies and Surro Fairies.

Vanessa swiped her phone screen. She skipped over fairy after fairy, but she kept saying, "I don't know. Maybe the next one."

But then she stopped on one little fairy with a pink dress. "Chrissie Surro... let's see, she loves to gather wishes from parents-to-be, loves to carry little embies until they grow into babies, she loves to laugh and tell jokes..."

"Sounds like someone I know," said Noah with a smile.

"She's so sweet and helpful," said Vanessa. "I think I've found our Surro Fairy."

In Surro Fairy Land, a few extra wishes came in at the last moment.

Chrissie Surro, always excited for new emby wishes, tumbled through the air. She fell at the feet of Maribel Surro, who arched an eyebrow.

"You really have to be more careful, Chrissie," she said. "Now let me see those extra wishes, please."

Maribel reviewed their wishes. They were from Vanessa and Noah... and another couple, Hugo and Peter: two more embies were needed.

Chrissie Surro raised her hand, jumping up and down. "I'm a Surro, too," she said. "Can I carry an emby?"

Maribel nodded. "Yes, you may, Chrissie Surro. We need a little baby girl for Vanessa and Noah."

Vanessa and Noah sat in front of their phone, watching a video of Chrissie Surro flying around. "We're almost ready here, folks." She pointed to a team of fairies who wore blue medical scrubs and purple gloves.

"This is our Surro Fairy Medical Team," said Maribel Surro.

She put on her glasses and flew in front of the camera. "They will look after our Surro Fairies and your new little embies. They'll help our loveable fairies create a warm home for their new womb-mates, the embies."

For the next few months, Vanessa and Noah, along with friends Hugo and Peter, received updates about their Surro Fairies as they ate healthy meals, took naps, and played peaceful fairy games like *"Catch the Sparkle"* and *"Where's the Brownie?"*

As the ninth month rolled around, the families-to-be had so many videos and pictures of their loveable Surro Fairies, they hardly knew what to do with them.

Vanessa and Hugo were so nervous and excited, but Noah and Peter, the calmer of the four, made sure to comfort them and show them pictures of their Surro Fairies.

Chrissie Surro fluttered her wings. "It's almost time for emby to become a baby!" She loved this time. "I can't wait to show Vanessa and Noah their new baby girl."

All the Surro Fairies were fluttering their wings and smiling and laughing. Sparkles and fairy dust filled the air.

Chrissie Surro giggled as she felt her belly. "Can you feel? She's kicking. She's ready to meet her new mommy and daddy."

Soon, Maribel Surro began to arrange the big days. She made appointments with midwives and doctors at hospitals. For the entire day, Maribel was on her fairy-phone, busy with calls.

Finally, she said, "Surro Fairies, it's that time again. We're going to have a special day. Let's get ready to fly down and let our parents meet their new babies."

A warm golden glow lit up Surro Fairy Land as the fairies flew into the air.

11

At the hospital, Vanessa and Noah were nervous, but when they saw Chrissie Surro fly in, they sighed with relief.

"She's healthy as a healthy fairy can be!" said the midwife. "It's almost time."

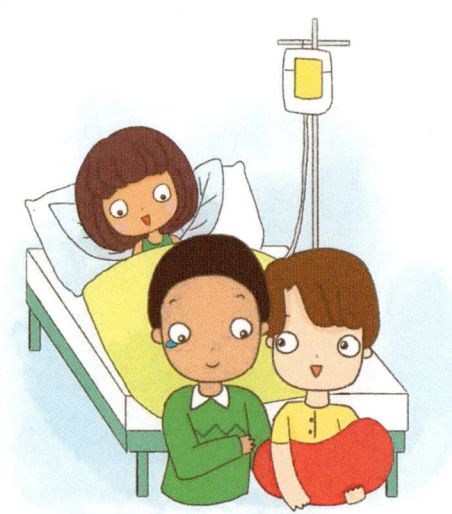

Everyone gathered around, and within a few minutes, a new baby girl was in the room. Chrissie Surro, the lovely fairy who'd carried her, hugged her and handed her to Vanessa and Noah.

There were a few tears to be sure, and lots of hugs and laughter.

Vanessa and Noah named their baby Lucy. Hugo and Peter named their baby boy Zachary.

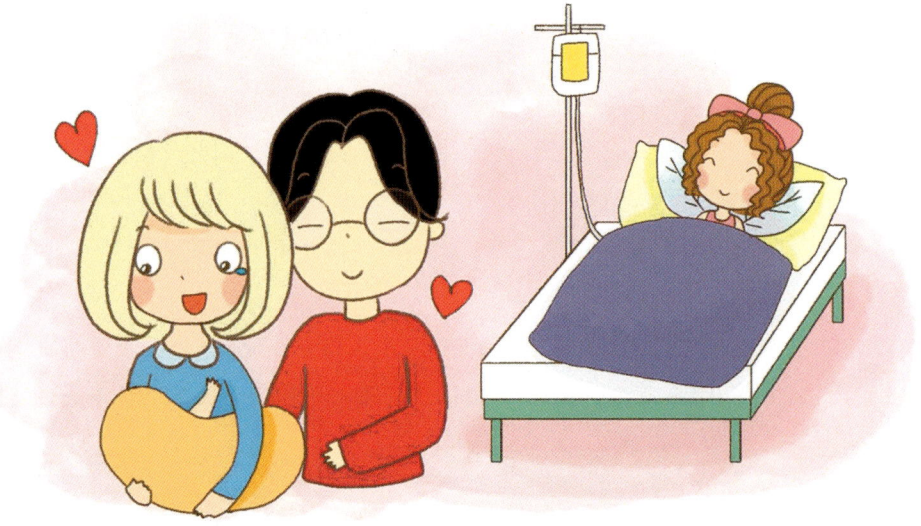

The two families kept in touch with their Surro Fairies and always told people their incredible stories.

And the Surro Fairies continued to gather wishes from mommies and daddies. Chrissie Surro still tumbled through the air, excited as ever, and Maribel Surro scribbled down every wish, so nobody was forgotten.

The End

Meet Chrissie

Hi! I'm Chrissie.
I'm a cheerful fairy from Surro Fairy Land.

I love helping mommies and daddies grow their families with beautiful babies just like you.
I get really excited when wishes arrive.
My fairy friends and I enjoy making everything extra special.

Always remember that if you believe in wishes strongly enough, they'll come true!

Meet Vanessa, Noah, Hugo, and Peter

Vanessa, Noah, Hugo, and Peter have been friends for a long time. Each family wanted to have their own babies but they were having a hard time doing so.

Fortunately, Noah found out about the Surro Fairies. Both couples were delighted and sent in their wishes. They were all happy that their baby's Lucy and Zachary could become friends too!

Meet Maribel

Maribel is a special fairy that takes care of organizing all of the wishes. She does a lot of talking with other fairies as well as mommies and daddies to make sure everything is just right.

You can catch her anytime flying around Surro Fairy Land with her tablet and wand. Her favorite game is *Catch the Sparkle*.

Wishes from Mommy or Daddy

_____

_____

_____

_____

_____

Michelle is a Life and Leadership Coach supporting families throughout the surrogacy community. She has earned certifications as a Co-Active Professional Certified Coach (CPCC) through the accredited Coaches Training Institute (CTI) and as an Associate Certified Coach (ACC) through the International Coaches Federation (ICF).

As a tribute to her late father, Michelle's passion for giving back paved her path to having ventured on her own journey where she became a surrogate and delivered healthy twins in the summer of 2018.

The Surro Fairy children's book came to fruition because of Michelle's own experiences and deep rooted passion for education. In her pursuit of increased awareness and support around surrogacy, the creation of the Surro Fairy™ brand came to life.

Surro Fairy's mission is to be a part of every story by supporting and celebrating surrogates and intended parents as they go through different phases of their journeys.

Follow us to stay connected with Surro Fairy

www.surrofairy.com

Made in the USA
Columbia, SC
18 November 2019